The essential
IELTS PREPARATION BOOK

ELS PAPERBACK

Table of Contents

1.1 Ielts : The Exam Tips

1.2 Easy ways to improve and expand your vocabulary

2.1 Academic Task 1 : (includes pie charts, bar charts; line graphs, maps, tables, Diagrams)

2.2 Answers Of Task 1

3.1 Academic Task 2 : Essays

3.2 Answers Of Task 2

4.1 Transition Words

4.2 Conjonctions

4.3 Introduction To Idiomatic expressions

4.4 Idiomatic Bank :

Ielts Band Scores

IELTS Sample Charts (IELTS Writing Task 1)

The Writing Task 1 of the IELTS Academic test requires you to write a summary of at least 150 words in response to a particular graph (bar, line or pie graph), table, chart, or process (how something works, how something is done). This task tests your ability to select and report the main features, to describe and compare data, identify significance and trends in factual information, or describe a process.

You are assessed on

- Task Achievement (how well you answer the question)
- Coherence and Cohesion
- Lexical Resource (use of appropriate vocabulary)
- Grammatical Range and Accuracy (the accuracy and range of the grammar you use)

Task 2 or Task 1 first ?

Students frequently ask whether they should do Task 1 first or Task 2. This obviously depends on the individual. It is probably wise, however, to do Task 1 first. From the psychological point of view, it gives you a sense of accomplishment when you have finished it.

Note that the value of the marks given to each Task is reflected in the time. There are twice as many marks for Task 2 as for Task 1. The marks are combined to produce one Band Score from 1 to 9 for the whole test. Note also that if you write less than 150 words for Task 1 and less than 250 for Task 2, you will lose marks.

IELTS Writing Task 1 Review

What information is Writing Task 1 based on?
Data presented as a table, graph (bar or pie chart) or a diagram.

How do you have to express the information?
Concisely and accurately.

Does it matter whether you use an informal style?
You should not use an informal style; you should write in a formal and academic style.

Are grammar, spelling and punctuation tested?
Yes, you should make sure you use a range of grammatical structures and try to be accurate.

How long should you spend on this task?
About 20 minutes.

How many words must you write?
At least 150.

Which parts of the data must you write about?
The most important or noticeable features, trends or points.

Should you make comparisons?
Yes, when appropriate.

What should you draw attention to and interpret?
Features of the data.

IELTS Writing Tip

Write a brief introduction in your own words using information from the question and the headings or text. For example, include an overview statement about what the data shows. After that, you should focus on key trends, main features and details. Every main feature should be supported by figures from the data. The report should finish with a short summary.

Do not speculate or offer an opinion that is outside the given data. Also, you do not need to describe every single change shown in the data, but describe the overall trends. General observations must be supported with specific examples from the data.

Use a variety of language to describe trends - for example, verbs with adverbs and nouns with adjectives. The examiner will want to see whether you can deal with the task with flexibility and precision. Showing your ability to use a wide range of vocabulary accurately and appropriately will help you get a higher score for your writing.

Do not copy the wording in the exam question. If you do, these words will be deducted from the total number of words and will not be assessed.

Easy ways to improve and expand your vocabulary

Seven Tips for Learning New Words

Communicate (speak and write) more clearly and concisely using these seven tips for learning new words... easy ways to improve and expand your vocabulary.
by Randall S. Hansen, Ph.D.
Looking for tips for improving your vocabulary? Whether you are trying to strengthen and broaden your vocabulary for school or personal growth, the key is a commitment to regularly learning new words.
Why expand your knowledge and use of words? You'll be able to communicate (speak and write) more clearly and concisely, people will understand you more easily, and you will increase the perception (and reality) that you are an intelligent person. Besides, learning new words is a fun activity -- and one you can even do with the people around you. Challenge a friend, family member, or roommate to learn new words with you.
This article reviews seven easy ways to improve your vocabulary and learn new words.

1. Read, read, and read. The more you read -- especially novels and literary works, but also magazines and newspapers -- the more words you'll be exposed to. As you read and uncover new words, use a combination of attempting to derive meaning from the context of the sentence as well as from looking up the definition in a dictionary.

2. Keep a dictionary and thesaurus handy. Use whatever versions you prefer -- in print, software, or online. When you uncover a new word, look it up in the dictionary to get both its pronunciation and its meaning(s). Next, go to the thesaurus and find similar words and phrases -- and their opposites (synonyms and antonyms, respectively) -- and learn the nuances among the words.

3. Use a journal. It's a good idea to keep a running list of the new words you discover so that you can refer back to the list and slowly build them into your everyday vocabulary. Plus, keeping a journal of all your new words can provide positive reinforcement for learning even more words -- especially when you can see how many new words you've already learned.

4. Learn a word a day. Using a word-a-day calendar or Website -- or developing your own list of words to learn -- is a great technique many people use to learn new words. This approach may be too rigid for some, so even if you do use this method, don't feel you must learn a new word every day. (Find some word-a-day Websites at the end of this article.)

5. Go back to your roots. One of the most powerful tools for learning new words -- and for deciphering the meaning of other new words -- is studying Latin and Greek roots. Latin and Greek elements (prefixes, roots, and suffixes) are a significant part of the English language and a great tool for learning new words. (Follow these links for the sections of this site that provide English Vocabulary Derived from Latin and English Vocabulary Derived from Greek.)

6. Play some games. Word games that challenge you and help you discover new meanings and new words are a great and fun tool in your quest for expanding your vocabulary. Examples include crossword puzzles, anagrams, word jumble, Scrabble, and Boggle. (Find some word-game Websites at the end of this article.)

7. Engage in conversations. Simply talking with other people can help you learn discover new words. As with reading, once you hear a new word, remember to jot it down so that you can study it later -- and then slowly add the new word to your vocabulary.

Final Thoughts On Improving and Expanding Your Vocabulary

You hold the key to a better vocabulary. By using the tips outlined , you should be well on your way to discovering and learning new words to expand your vocabulary and strengthen your use of the English language.

Finally, remember that you must practice putting your new words into your writing and speaking or risk not retaining them in your brain. Use repetition exercises when you first learn a word -- and consider other learning techniques, such as index cards, recording yourself reciting your words, association games, and mnemonics.

ACADEMIC
TASK 1

Academic Task 1: Table #1 (Answered)

Top ten countries with largest population, in million

2019		2100 projection	
China	1,439	India	1,551
India	1,380	China	941
USA	331	Nigeria	730
Indonesia	274	USA	478
Pakistan	221	Pakistan	316
Brazil	213	D.R. Congo*	296
Nigeria	206	Indonesia	292
Bangladesh	165	Ethiopia	212
Russia	146	Tanzania	178
Mexico	129	Brazil	177

*Democratic Republic of Congo

You should spend about 20 minutes on this task.

The table below shows top ten countries with largest population in 2019, and how it is projected to change by 2100.
Summarise the information by selecting and reporting the main features, and make comparisons where relevant.

Write at least 150 words.

Exam tip: Writing an introduction
Use the following structure for the introduction to a Task 1 answer:

One sentence to explain what the table shows. (Use different words from the words used in the heading for the table wherever possible.)
One or two sentences summarizing the information shown in the table. Do not include details in the introduction. Save the details for the main part of your text, after the introduction

Academic Task 1: Bar Chart #2 (Answered)

You should spend about 20 minutes on this task.

The diagrams below show the main reasons workers chose to work from home and the hours males and females worked at home for the year 2019.

Summarise the information by selecting and reporting the main features, and make comparisons where relevant.

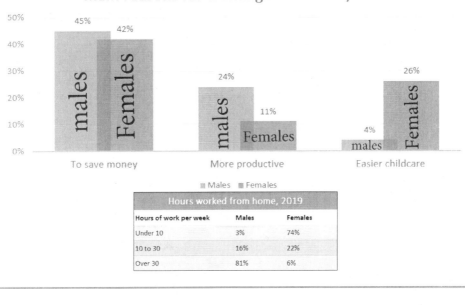

Main reasons for working from home, 2019

Hours worked from home, 2019

Hours of work per week	Males	Females
Under 10	3%	74%
10 to 30	16%	22%
Over 30	81%	6%

Exam tip
Remember that some repetition is acceptable and can even be effective as a means of signposting key ideas. If you do not know suitable synonyms for some key terms, it is better to repeat these words than to use expressions that are a poor match or inappropriate to the context.

Academic Task 1: Bar Chart #3

You should spend about 20 minutes on this task.

The bar chart below gives information about the percentage of the population living in urban areas in different parts of the world.

Summarise the information by selecting and reporting the main features, and make comparisons where relevant.

Write at least 150 words.

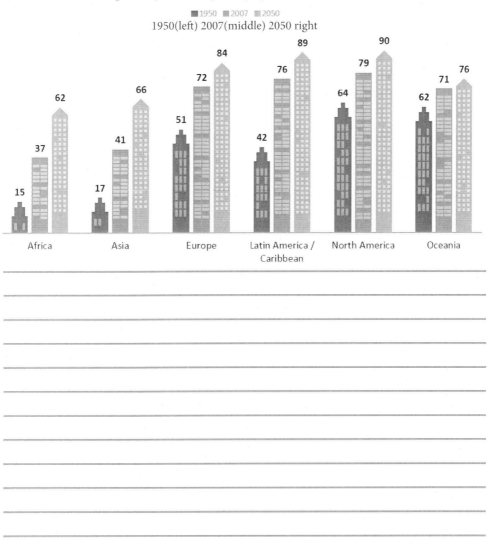

Identifying and comparing data on a chart

Some texts include statistics and data in graphical form. To understand this information, first identify:

1/ the title of the chart
2/ the title of each axis (horizontal and vertical)
3/ the label of each category, represented by a column, row or line in the chart
4/ the units of measurement for each axis (e.g. time, numbers, percentages, distances)
5/ the values for each category
6/ the legend (the colour or pattern assigned to each category in the chart

Academic Task 1: Diagram #4

You should spend about 20 minutes on this task.

The diagrams below give information about the manufacture of frozen fish pies.
Summarise the information by selecting and reporting the main features, and make comparisons where relevant.

Write at least 150 words.

A fish pie

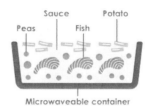

Fish pie production line

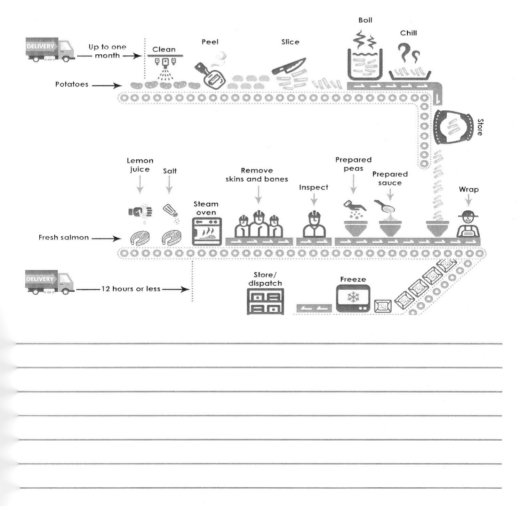

IELTS Writing Task 1: Describing a Process or an Object

Although interpreting and presenting data is the most common task type for Task 1 of the Writing module, two other tasks are possible. In one, you are given a diagram and asked to describe a process or to explain how something works. In the other, you have to describe an object or a series of events.

You might be required to describe an object and how it works or describe and compare two or more objects. This type of task is less common.

Academic Task 1: Line Graph #5 (Answered)

You should spend about 20 minutes on this task.

The graph below gives information about how much people in the United States and the United Kingdom spend on fuel.

Summarise the information by selecting and reporting the main features, and make comparisons where relevant.

Write at least 150 words.

How much do people spend on fuel?

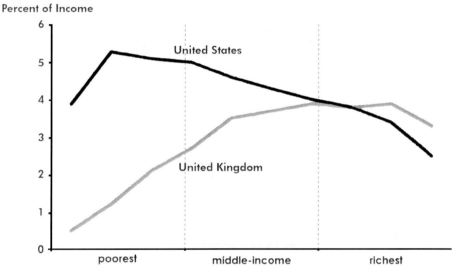

Source: Smith 1992. Chermick and Reschovsky 1997.

Writing about graphs

When writing about graphs, look at the visual information overall without focusing on the details. You will usually be able to identify three or four main trends or patterns. Circle or draw arrows on the graph to highlight the key features and patterns. Consider: upward and downward movements, highest and lowest points and the start and end points for the range of information shown. Identifying key trends will help you structure your writing

Academic Task 1: Table #6

You should spend about 20 minutes on this task.

The table below shows the results of surveys in 2005, 2010 and 2015 about McGill University.

Summarise the information by selecting and reporting the main features, and make comparisons where relevant.

Write at least 150 words.

	2005	2010	2015
Teaching quality	74	72	78
Library resources	86	88	87
Student services	54	81	95
Range of modules offered	39	31	25
Sports and social facilities	65	65	65

IELTS TIPS

Make sure you understand exactly what the visual shows. You get this key information from two sources: the first sentence of the task itself and the title of the visual(s).

Start with an introductory sentence which summarises what the visual shows. Don't simply copy down what's in the question, this is a waste of your time.

Academic Task 1: Line Graph #7

You should spend about 20 minutes on this task.

The graph shows the impact of vaccinations on the incidence of whooping cough, a childhood illness, between 1940 and 1990 in Britain.

Summarise the information by selecting and reporting the main features, and make comparisons where relevant.

Write at least 150 words

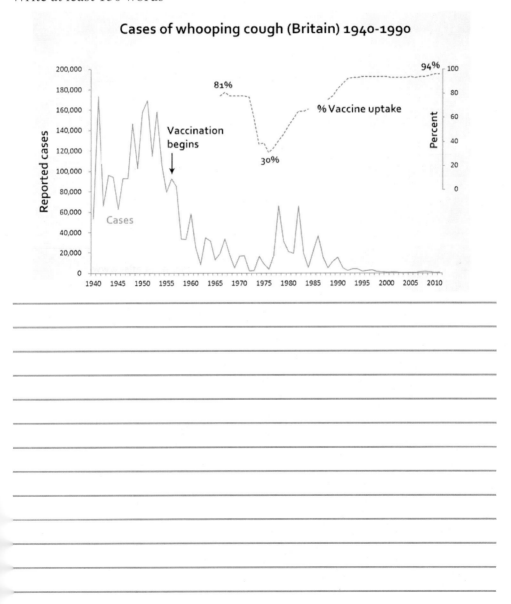

IELTS Tip

If you are presented with two figures which appear to show a cause and effect relationship, it is helpful to take note of this. It will enable you to highlight the information more effectively. However, you should be cautious about expressing a cause and effect relationship too directly. This is because IELTS Writing Task 1 does not ask you to interpret the graph or refer to anything outside of it. If you use a cause and effect expression (e.g. causes, leads to), use a hedging expression to make the claim less sweeping (e.g. appears to cause, may lead to)

Academic Task 1: Bar Chart #8

You should spend about 20 minutes on this task.

The bar chart gives information about the number of car journeys into the city centre made by residents and non-residents.

Summarise the information by selecting and reporting the main features, and make comparisons where relevant.

Write at least 150 words.

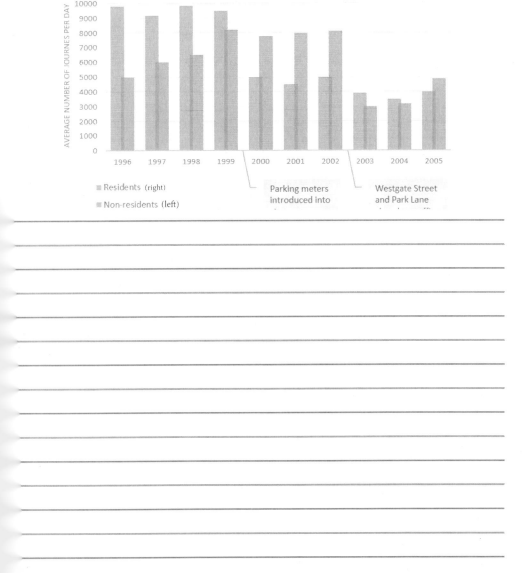

INFO

For Writing Task 1 you may have to describe and compare two or more charts, graphs or tables. These may show information about the same topic but focus on different aspects.

You will need to understand what information each chart / graph / table shows and find the relationships between them. For example, you may need to notice a change in one table / chart / graph that could be caused or be the cause of a change in another table / chart / graph.

Academic Task 1: Table #9

You should spend about 20 minutes on this task.

The table below shows the percentage use of four different fuel types to generate electricity in five Asian countries in 2005.

Summarise the information by selecting and reporting the main features, and make comparisons where relevant.

Write at least 150 words.

	Nuclear	Coal & lignite	Petroleum products	Hydro & wind	Other
Malaysia	19	61	2	5	13
Singapore	13	42	3	3	39
Thailand	0	3	36	19	42
South Korea	33	5	3	48	11
Japan	49	6	3	3	39

IELTS TIP

Whether you have to describe a graph, table or chart, think carefully about what you need to include in your description. Don't describe every detail of the information. Choose the most important and interesting features to write about.

Support your description with figures, but you don't need to give every number exactly. You can be approximate by using words like 'over', 'about' and 'around'.

Academic Task 1: Line Graph #10 (Answered)

You should spend about 20 minutes on this task.

The graph below gives information about changes in the birth and death rates in New Zealand between 1901 and 2101.

Summarise the information by selecting and reporting the main features, and make comparisons where relevant.

Write at least 150 words.

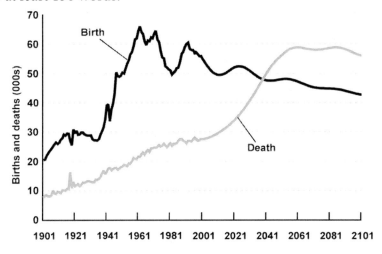

Using the right tenses

It is important to select the correct tenses. Points to remember:

For most visuals a specific time in the past will be given and you will need to use the past simple tense. If two things took place at the same time, you may use the past continuous tense for one of them. (While poultry production was rising during this period, there was no change in mutton production).

If you use since or recent(ly) it means that you are referring to events that have come up to the present. That means using the present perfect tense. (The use of the Internet has risen enormously since the 1990s.)
With by you will often need to use the past perfect or the future perfect tense. (By the end of the century the rate of urbanisation had doubled.)

Academic Task 1: Diagram #11

You should spend about 20 minutes on this task.

The diagram below shows the recycling process of aluminium cans.

Summarise the information by selecting and reporting the main features, and make comparisons where relevant.

Write at least 150 words.

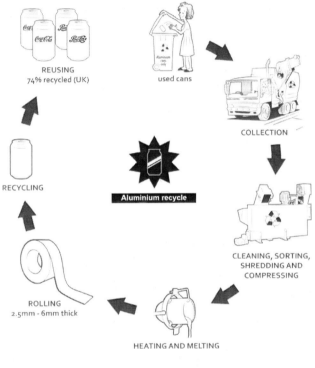

Useful language

In the introduction you can use: The diagram/picture/chart shows/illustrates/describes/depicts the process of/how …

Find a starting point and write the process as a series of steps.

Useful connecting words you can use are:

  Adverbs: first/firstly/first of all, secondly, thirdly, then/next/after that/following that/ following on from this/subsequently/subsequent to that, finally

  Prepositions: At the beginning of …; At the end of …

Use the present simple to describe processes.

The agent is not usually mentioned unless a task is performed by a particular person.

When describing a cycle, you can conclude: The cycle then repeats itself/is then repeated

Academic Task 1: Pie Chart #12 (Answered)

You should spend about 20 minutes on this task.

The charts below show local government expenditure in 2010 and 2015. Summarise the information by selecting and reporting the main features, and make comparisons where relevant.

Write at least 150 words.

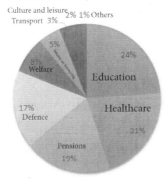

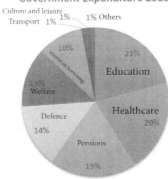

Strategies for IELTS Writing Task 1

-Work out how many lines 150 words are in your handwriting, e.g. if you write about 10 words per line, then you will need to produce at least 15 lines. Aim to write no more than 170/180 words.

-Check that you have written at least 150 words. If you write less, it will affect your score.

-Compare general trends, differences, etc. and support this with information from the diagram. Avoid focusing too closely on the details.

-If you have more than one graph or chart or mixture, link the information.

-Make sure you write in paragraphs: an introduction, one or two paragraphs for the body of the text. Then write a brief conclusion

Academic Task 1: Line graph #13

You should spend about 20 minutes on this task.

The diagram below shows a possible future means of home energy production.

Summarise the information by selecting and reporting the main features, and make comparisons where relevant.

Write at least 150 words

Strategies for IELTS Writing Task 1

Rather than trying to give reasons for the elements shown in the diagram or describing every detail, concentrate only on significant features.

Your description should start with a brief overview of the object(s) and its purpose.

Then focus on how the object works or significant similarities and differences between the objects.

Vary your language where possible, and use a range of vocabulary and structures.

Your description should end with a summarising statement.

Academic Task 1: Table #14

You should spend about 20 minutes on this task.

The table below gives information about student enrolments at Manchester University in 1937, 1967 and 2017.

Summarise the information by selecting and reporting the main features, and make comparisons where relevant.

Write at least 150 words.

Manchester University student enrolments			
	1937	1967	2017
How many new students enrolled?	327	1133	6254
What percentage were female?	45%	35%	55%
What percentage were male?	55%	65%	45%
What percentage came from within 40 miles of Manchester?	55%	15%	1-2%
What percentage came from oversease?	6% from 4 countries	7% from 26 coutries	32% from 102 countries

Line graphs

A line graph shows how the value of something changes over time. The vertical axis shows quantities, e.g. numbers, percentages or money. The horizontal axis shows different points in time, usually months or years. Different quantities measured at different points in time can be joined using a continuous line to show a trend or how these quantities change, e.g. increase, decrease, or stay the same. More lines (different colours or styles) can be used for different categories. The key explains which categories are being measured.

Do word puzzles and games like crosswords, anagrams and wordsearches. Make word cards and take them with you. Read them on the bus or when you are waiting for your friends.

Academic Task 1: Bar chart #15

You should spend about 20 minutes on this task.

The chart below shows the places visited by different people living in Canada.
Summarise the information by selecting and reporting the main features, and make comparisons where relevant.

Write at least 150 words.

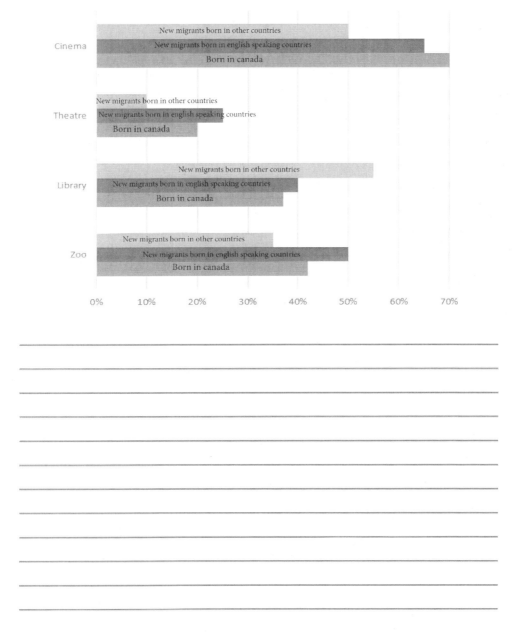

IELTS Tip

For the IELTS Writing Task 1 you have to summarize information that is usually represented in the form of a table, a pie chart, a line graph, a bar chart, a diagram, a map or a flow chart.

You should write at least 150 words and organize your work carefully into three separate parts:

1) An opening paragraph briefly describing what the graph or figure shows (1-3 sentences)

2) Body paragraph(s) highlighting the key information

3) A concluding paragraph summarizing the most important point (1-2 sentences)

Academic Task 1: Bar chart #16

You should spend about 20 minutes on this task.

The chart below gives information about the number of social networking sites people used in Canada in 2014 and 2015.

Summarise the information by selecting and reporting the main features, and make comparisons where relevant.

Write at least 150 words.

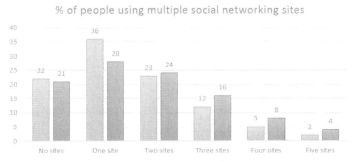

% of people using multiple social networking sites

2014 Left Bars - 2015 Right Bars

TEST Tip
Make sure your headphones are working , if not make sure they will replace them for you

Academic Task 1: Table #17

You should spend about 20 minutes on this task.

The table below gives information about UK independent films.

Summarise the information by selecting and reporting the main features, and make comparisons where relevant.

Write at least 150 words

Independent films released in the UK and Republic of Ireland by genre 2012			
Genre	Number of releases	% of all releases	% of income from ticket sales
Comedy	26	17.6	45.4
Horror	14	9.5	20.2
Biopic	1	0.7	9.1
Drama	35	23.6	8.3
Crime	7	4.7	4.7
Action	4	2.7	4.1
Documentary	35	23.6	2.9
Thriller	13	8.8	1.3
Romance	5	3.4	0.8
Other	8	5.4	3.2
Total	148	100	100

IELTS TIP
You can use either American or British spelling.

Academic Task 1: Bar Chart #18

You should spend about 20 minutes on this task.

The charts summarise the weight measurements of people living in Charlestown in 1955 and 2015.

Summarise the information by selecting and reporting the main features, and make comparisons where relevant.

Write at least 150 words.

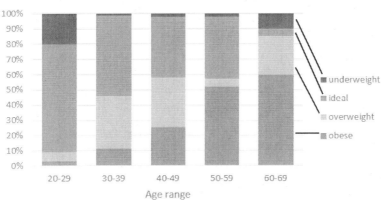

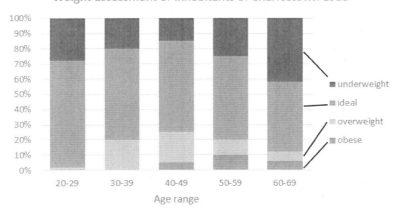

IELTS Tip

Be careful of the following common errors when describing changes in numbers.

1/ There was an increase of 20% between 1955 and 2015. NOT an increase in 20%

2/ There was an increase in obesity between 1955 and 2015. NOT increase of obesity

Academic Task 1: Map #19 (Answered)

You should spend about 20 minutes on this task.

The maps below show the changes that have taken place at Queen Mary Hospital since its construction in 1960.

Summarise the information by selecting and reporting the main features, and make comparisons where relevant.

Write at least 150 words

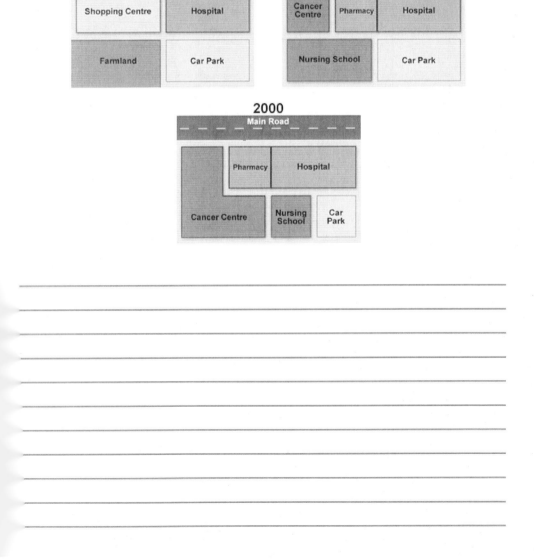

IELTS Tip

Note that the number of words in this sample is 178(answer). Always write at least 150 words but do not go much over this figure as you will not get any extra marks and you will use up time which you can better spend on doing Task 2.

Academic Task 1: Line Graph #20

You should spend about 20 minutes on this task.

The line graph below shows the percentage of tourists to England who visited four different attractions in Brighton.

Summarise the information by selecting and reporting the main features, and make comparisons where relevant.

Write at least 150 words.

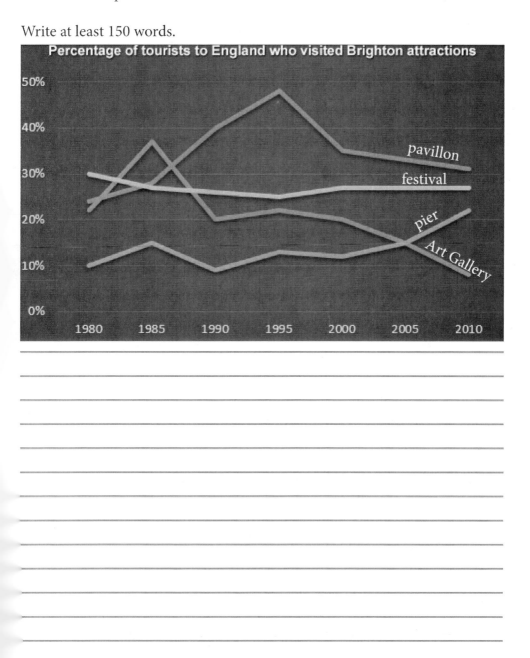

IELTS Tip: Useful language for describing trends

- to experience a(n) [increase/decrease/rise/fall/drop in/of]
- to [increase/decrease/rise/fall/drop by/from … to]
- to fluctuate / undergo a change / remain [stable/steady] / stagnate / dip - / peak / increase [twofold/threefold] / surge
- a [less/more] marked [increase/decrease], etc. (occurred / took place)
- [less/more] significant / steady / especially strong growth
- a parallel [rise/fall]
- to expect / predict / forecast
- express opinions (views, complaints etc.)

Academic Task 1: Diagram #21

You should spend about 20 minutes on this task.

The diagram below shows the production of electricity using a system called Ocean Thermal Energy Conversion (OTEC).

Write a report for a university lecturer describing the information below.

Write at least 150 words.

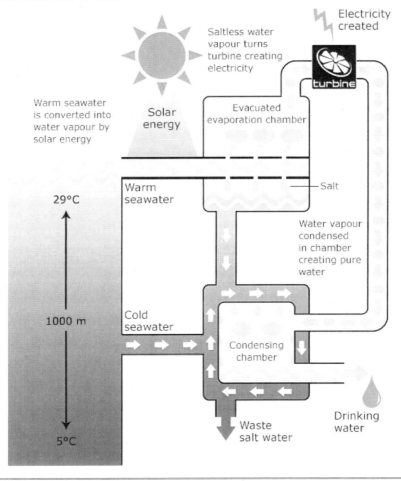

Test Tip

For IELTS Task 1 you may have to describe a physical process. This may be illustrated in the form of a diagram showing the different steps or stages in the process.

Using the present simple passive forms of verbs relevant to the process is the key to getting a high score for process diagram. The examiner will give you a mark for Grammatical Range and Accuracy, and correctly

Academic Task 1: Table #22 (Answered)

You should spend about 20 minutes on this task.

The Table below shows the results of a survey that asked 6800 Scottish adults (aged 16 years and over) whether they had taken part in different cultural activities in the past 12 months.

Summarise the information by selecting and reporting the main features, and make comparisons where relevant.

Write at least 150 words.

Participation in cultural activities, by age

	16-24	25-44	45-74	All aged 16 and over
	%	%	%	%
Any performance*	35	22	17	22
Undertaking any crafts	11	17	22	19
Cultural purchases	11	17	18	16
Any visual arts	30	16	11	15
Any writing	17	6	5	7
Computer based	10	9	5	6

* Dancing, singing, playing musical instruments and acting

IELTS TIP

-Begin with an introductory statement, e.g. The table/graph shows…
-Don't try to describe every detail. Look for significant features, e.g. the biggest change, the overall trend, etc.
-Don't speculate about reasons for trends. Stick to the facts.
-End with a comment on general trends, e.g. From this evidence we can conclude that…

Academic Task 1: Map #23

You should spend about 20 minutes on this task.

The map below is of the town of Canterbury. A new school (S) is planned for the area. The map shows two possible sites for the school.

Summarise the information by selecting and reporting the main features, and make comparisons where relevant.

Write at least 150 words

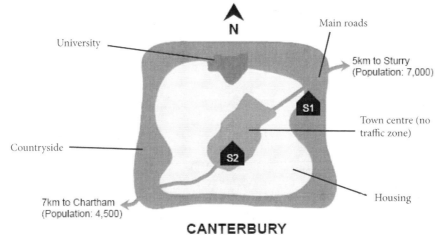

CANTERBURY

IELTS Tip

The majority of Task 1 questions in the IELTS exam are either a graph with trends or a graph with comparatives. However, there are two other possible types of questions:

Describing a process (for example, how to produce chocolate)
Describing a map (often of a city in two time periods)

Academic Task 1: Pie Chart And Table #24

You should spend about 20 minutes on this task.

The diagrams below give information on transport and car use in Edmonton.

Summarise the information by selecting and reporting the main features, and make comparisons where relevant.

Write at least 150 words

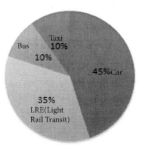

People's reasons for using the car in city

Commute to work   55%
Shopping   15%
Leisure activities   15%
Taking children to school   40%
Business   45%

In IELTS Writing Task 1, when you must describe two figures, ask yourself the following:

1/ What do both figures relate to?
2/ What kind of relationship is evident? (a similarity, a difference, a cause and effect relationship or some other type of relationship)
3/ Which aspects of each figure should be highlighted?
4/ Should I describe the figures in separate paragraphs, or should I compare different aspects of the figures within a series of paragraph?

Academic Task 1: #25 (Answered)

You should spend about 20 minutes on this task.

The graphs below provide information on global population figures and figures for urban populations in different world regions.

Summarise the information by selecting and reporting the main features, and make comparisons where relevant.

Write at least 150 words

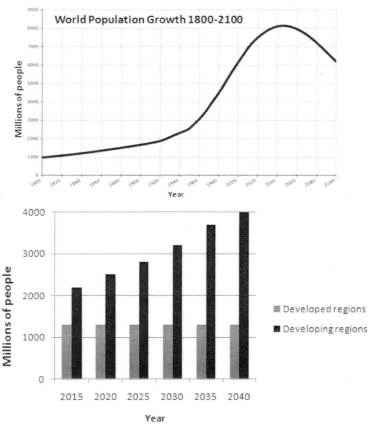

Test Tip

If there is more than one diagram, study any heading, key or source for each. Decide what the vertical and horizontal axes measure, and what the bars show. Look for similarities, differences, changes and trends.

Sometimes in the exam you can be asked to write about a graph with future trend. You should write your answer in the same way as before, but instead of using the past simple, change the grammar and use future tenses.

ANSWERS :

TASK 1 #1 MODEL ANSWER

The table compares the population of the world's top ten countries in 2019 with projected numbers in 2100.

In 2019, China had the highest population of 1,439 million, with India second on 1,380 million. However, by 2100, India is projected to have the highest population of 1,551 million with China second on 941 million - down 498 million since 2019. Although the USA is projected to increase its population from 331 million to 478 million, it steps down from third to fourth place, being overtaken by Nigeria, which moves up from seventh place with 206 million, to a total of 730 million, representing a massive increase of 524 million. Brazil drops from sixth place in 2019 with 213 million, down to tenth in 2100 on 177 million - a decrease of 36 million.

Three of the ten most populous countries in the world will no longer be among the top ten in 2100, and all three will be supplanted by rapidly growing nations in Africa.

Except for China and Brazil, all other projections show an increase between 2019 and 2100, but there is a significant shuffling of position by some countries, the elimination of others, and the introduction of new contenders for a top-ten placing

(203 words)

TASK 1 #2 MODEL ANSWER

The bar chart illustrates the reasons men and women chose to work from home in 2019. Overall, saving money was the main reason for both males and females (45% and 42% respectively). In contrast, approximately a quarter of males put productivity as a reason, which was twice as high as the female response (24% and 11% respectively). For childcare, the pattern was different again with almost a quarter of females giving this reason compared to very few males (4%).

The table shows the hours men and women worked from home in 2019. The vast majority of males worked over 30 hours per week (81%) contrasting with a minority of females (6%) doing similar hours. This pattern is reversed when examining the under ten hours category with almost three quarters of females working this amount compared to only 3% of males. The 10 to 30 hours per week category shows fewer marked differences.

To sum up, it can be seen that men and women do not always give the same reasons for home working and, in general, men work longer hours from home.

(182 words)

TASK 1 #5 BAND 9 ANSWER

The graph compares the percentage income that people in the UK and USA spend on fuel.

Firstly, the difference between the total spending on fuel by the poorest and the richest is greater in the UK than in the USA. In the former, the poorest spend less than 0.5% of their income on fuel, suggesting that they do not use cars very much, and the richest spend around 3%. By contrast, in the US, the poorest spend around 4-5% while the richest spend between 2 and 3%.

Secondly, in the USA it is also noticeable that the percentage of income spent by the poor can be twice that spent by the rich. However, in the UK. the percentage spent rises quite steeply for the poorer members of the population but then remains almost constant apart from the very richest, where it falls again.

In both countries people on middle incomes spend about the same percentage. Overall, the percentage of income spent on fuel generally gets higher in the UK, whereas it decreases in the US.

(175 words)

TASK 1 #10 BAND 9 ANSWER

The graph shows changes in the birth and death rates in New Zealand since 1901, and forecasts trends tip until 2101.

Between 1901 and the present day, the birth rate has been consistently higher than the death rate. It stood at 20,000 at the start of this period and increased to a peak of 66,000 in 1961. Since then the rate has fluctuated between 65 and 50 thousand and it is expected to decline slowly to around 45,000 births by the end of the century.

In contrast, the death rate started below 10,000 and has increased steadily until the present time. This increase is expected to be more rapid between 2021 and 2051 when the rate will probably level off at around 60,000, before dropping slightly in 2101.

Overall, these opposing trends mean that the death rate will probably overtake the birth rate in around 2041 and the large gap between the two levels will be reversed in the later part of this century.

164 words)

TASK 1 #12 SAMPLE BAND 9 ANSWER

The charts show the percentage breakdown of government spending across nine categories in 2010 and 2015. Over the five-year period, there were significant changes in expenditure.

In both years, the four largest areas of government expenditure were: education, healthcare, pensions, and defence, with education taking the largest share (24% in 2010 and 21% in 2015). The smallest areas of expenditure were transport, culture and leisure and "other". Interest on borrowing and spending on welfare lay in between.

Interestingly, between 2010 and 2015, spending on all four of the largest areas had dropped, with the exception of pensions, which remained the same at 19%. Spending on transport and culture and leisure also fell significantly, with the transport budget declining by two thirds. On the other hand, spending on welfare and interest on government borrowing rose markedly, with the latter doubling over the five-year period to 10%.

Overall, the charts indicate that the government has had to cut expenditure in most areas in order to fund the cost of borrowing and welfare.

(170 words)

TASK 1 #19 SAMPLE BAND 9 ANSWER

The diagrams show Queen Mary Hospital at three different stages in its development: 1960, 1980 and 2000.

In 1960, the hospital was built close to a main road and next to a shopping centre. A large area behind the hospital was turned into a car park, while the area behind the shopping centre was farmland.

By 1980, the shopping centre had been demolished in order to make way for two additional hospital building which became a pharmacy and a cancer centre. Furthermore, the hospital gained the farmland and converted it into a nursing school.

In 2000, the main hospital building remained unchanged but the cancer centre was extended to cover the entire nursing school. As a result of this, the original car park was divided into two so that it provided a smaller car park and a small nursing school.

During this period, the hospital has increased in size and, in addition to a new nursing school, a cancer centre has been created and extended. Hence the capacity of the car park has been reduced by a half.

(178 words)

TASK 1 #22 SAMPLE BAND 9 ANSWER

The table shows details of participation in a variety of cultural activities over a year, according to the age of the participants.

Overall, any performance, which includes dancing, singing, playing musical instruments and acting, had the highest level of participation, with 22% of respondents participating in the previous 12 months. By contrast, computer based activities had the lowest level of participation (6 per cent).

People aged between 45 and 74 years old were most likely to undertake any activity to do with crafts (22 per cent), while performances were more likely to be participated in by those aged 16 to 24 (35 per cent). The differences between age groups were particularly marked in the case of visual arts and writing categories, where participation rates were around three times higher for younger people than for the older ones. It is clear from the evidence that age plays a significant role in the popularity of the cultural activities listed.

(157 words)

TASK 1 #25 SAMPLE BAND 9 ANSWER

The first graph shows the trend in world population growth between 1800 and 2100, while the second graph gives predicted urban population figures for the next 25 years.

The world population has experienced continuous growth since 1800. Between 1800 and 1950, the population grew slowly from just under 1 billion to 2.5 billion people. After that, the growth rate increased and currently the figure is around 6.5 billion. Projections show a continued increase in population in the near future, but a steady decline in the population growth rate. The global population is expected to peak at 8.2 billion by 2050, and then decline to around 6.2 billion by 2100.

The predictions also show that almost all urban population growth in the next 25 years will occur in cities of developing countries. In developed regions, on the other hand, the urban population is expected to remain unchanged at about 1.3 billion people over the next two decades.

The graphs show that the global population increase will not occur evenly throughout the world, but will be greater in some areas than others.

(180 words)

ACADEMIC
TASK 2

The essay for Task 2 of the IELTS writing exam is something that a lot of students are afraid of.

You must write about 250 words and this should be completed in approximately 40 minutes (because you also need to complete Writing Task 1 in the first 20 minutes of the 1 hour writing test).

To write the perfect answer and get the highest IELTS band score possible, you need to write quickly but also keep calm and focussed on writing your answer.

In all parts of the IELTS exam, you should try to show that you have a broad knowledge of English vocabulary, ensure that you write with correct spelling and avoid silly little grammar mistakes.

IELTS WRITING TASK 2 Best answer
The essay type questions for Task 2 are usually asking about some general thing in society. The topic could be education, health, age, gender roles, the youth, the environment... basically anything.

Therefore, you cannot learn an amazing sentence that you can insert into an essay, as it is very unlikely that you will be able to use it in your specific question that you have on the day of your test.

However, there is a system to use that gives you a great balanced structure which will help you get a good mark for answering the question... which is after all the whole point of this task - answer the question! Lots of IELTS candidates do not actually do this, as they are trying to impress the examiner with big posh words and forget to focus on actually giving a point of view and supporting that opinion with good examples and clear thought.

STEP 1: INTRODUCTION

Repeat the question in your own words

In the essay introduction, you should start by repeating the question. This does NOT mean that you should COPY the question.

You should say the question again, but using different words that mean the same thing (synonyms).
For example, if your question was something like: Some people believe that capital punishment should never be used. Others believe that it could be used for the most serious crimes. Discuss both views and give your opinion.

Then the opening sentence of your introduction should use synonyms to say the question again in your own words. for example: It is a commonly held belief that the death penalty is a Draconian penalty and not appropriate in modern society. However, there is also an argument that the most despicable crimes should have this most severe of punishments.

Now, don't worry about the high level of the example sentences above. I am a native English speaker and I am an English teacher, so the sentences should be good, shouldn't they?

But, from the example, you can see that it is possible to re-write the question using completely different vocabulary and still retain the original meaning and 'flavour' of the original question.

Give your opinion

As soon as you have restated the question, then give your opinion on the subject.
This gives the examiner an overview of what is to come in your essay.

It is important to note that it does not matter what your opinion is! There is no right or wrong answer to an IELTS essay question. You do NOT have to try and think "What will the examiner think is the right answer here". The examiner is only interested in the level of your English. So just give your first instinct opinion and don't try to out-think yourself.

STEP 2: Support your opinion

Now that you have given your opinion, you need to back it up.

The best way to do this is to give examples.

You can begin this paragraph with phrases like:

Personally, I believe that...
From my point of view...
I am convinced that...
In my opinion...
In my view...

So, if your opinion was that you are against capital punishment, then as an example you could write about situations where people have been jailed for life for murder and then decades later they have been released as they were proven to be innocent. The relevant vocabulary here is "a miscarriage of justice".

Your argument would be that when a miscarriage of justice occurs, the prisoner would most likely have faced the death penalty and would have been killed even though they were innocent.

Another example could be that many murders are committed in 'hot blood' and often as an 'act of passion'.. This means that the murder was so angry about something that they were not thinking properly

STEP 3: Give the other side of the argument

In your next paragraph, you should look at the question from the opposite viewpoint to yours.

This shows the examiner that you have balance in your writing and it is a sign of a good essay.

You can start this paragraph with phrases such as:

It can also be argued that…
Someone who held the opposing view would say that…
However, there is also another side to this discussion.
In contrast, some people hold the view that…

STEP 4: Conclusion - Summarise your opinion

To finish off your IELTS task 2 essay, you need to summarise your whole argument as a conclusion.

Essentially, this means that you give your opinion again that you stated in the introduction.

To prove to the IELTS examiner that you have a good command of English vocabulary you should try again to use synonyms and not just copy your previous sentence. Now, you can add your expanded arguments (from step 2) into your opinion.

A conclusion that weighs up the arguments already mentioned is a really good opportunity to use a conditional sentence.

If capital punishment was reintroduced into society, I do not believe that it would act as a deterrent for heinous crimes. It is my strongly held belief that the death penalty would only result in future miscarriages of justice that serve no purpose in civilised society.

IELTS Writing Task 2 #26

You should spend about 40 minutes on this task.

Write about the following topic:

In the past, shopping was a routine domestic task. Many people nowadays regard it as a hobby.

To what extent do you think this is a positive trend?

Give reasons for your answer and include any relevant examples from your own knowledge or experience.

Write at least 250 words.

Vocabulary Tip

The word staff refers to all the people working for an organisation. To talk about one person, you need to say member of staff or employee: I recently had a problem with a member of staff in your company (or an employee in your company or one of your staff). NOT I recently had a problem with a staff in your company

IELTS Writing Task 2 #27   (Answered)

You should spend about 40 minutes on this task.

Write about the following topic:

Supermarkets should only sell food produced from within their own country rather than imports from overseas.

What are your opinions on this?

Give reasons for your answer and include any relevant examples from your own knowledge or experience.

Write at least 250 words.

Exam Tip
Make sure that you address all the points in the question. Organise your ideas before you start to write and when you have finished, check your spelling and the number of words you have used.

IELTS Writing Task 2 #28

You should spend about 40 minutes on this task.

Write about the following topic:

In the modern world, the image (photograph or film) is becoming a more powerful way of communicating than the written word.

To what extent do you agree or disagree?

Give reasons for your answer and include any relevant examples from your own knowledge or experience.

Write at least 250 words.

Exam Tip

Make sure that you address all the points in the question. Organise your ideas before you start to write and when you have finished, check your spelling and the number of words you have used.

IELTS Writing Task 2 #29

You should spend about 40 minutes on this task.

Write about the following topic:

Longer life spans and improvements in the health of older people suggest that people over the age of sixty-five can continue to live full and active lives.

In what ways can society benefit from the contribution that older people can make?

Give reasons for your answer and include any relevant examples from your own knowledge or experience.

Write at least 250 words.

IELTS TIP

It is very important that you try to keep the word limits, and perhaps write just a little more. You could write between 150 and 180 words for Task 1 and 250 to 300 for Task 2. If you write too few words, you will lose marks. While practising for the IELTS exam, count the number of words you write per line and then work out how many lines you need to reach the 150/250 word limit. It may surprise you how little you have to write! You could draw a line to mark the word limits when you are writing your homework. This will help train you to keep to the limits and help you to focus on where you are going and what you are aiming for.

IELTS Writing Task 2 #30   (Answered)

You should spend about 40 minutes on this task.

Write about the following topic:

Car ownership has increased so rapidly over the past thirty years that many cities in the world are now 'one big traffic jam'.

How true do you think this statement is? What measures can governments take to discourage people from using their cars?

Give reasons for your answer and include any relevant examples from your own knowledge or experience.

Write at least 250 words

IELTS TIP

The exam is not testing knowledge of English language, but rather competence in using English. In other words, it is not testing memory. Awareness of this might help reduce some of the problems that many candidates have in the IELTS exam.

IELTS Writing Task 2 #31

You should spend about 40 minutes on this task.

Write about the following topic:

Increasing numbers of students are choosing to study abroad.

To what extent does this trend benefit the students themselves and the countries involved?

What are the drawbacks?

Give reasons for your answer and include any relevant examples from your own knowledge or experience.

Write at least 250 words.

IELTS TIP

Before you write
Read the task and make a mental summary of the key points and overall trends/stages.

IELTS Writing Task 2 #32

You should spend about 40 minutes on this task.

Write about the following topic:

Many people believe that the high levels of violence in films today are causing serious social problems.

What are these problems and how could they be reduced?

Give reasons for your answer and include any relevant examples from your own knowledge or experience.

Write at least 250 words.

IELTS TIP

As you write

Introduce the information, in a sentence or two, using your own words. Why? Because if you copy the question, the examiner will not count these words.

IELTS Writing Task 2 #33

You should spend about 40 minutes on this task.

Write about the following topic:

Women are better at childcare than men therefore they should focus more on raising children and less on their working life.

To what extent do you agree or disagree with this statement?

Give reasons for your answer and include any relevant examples from your own knowledge or experience.

Write at least 250 words.

IELTS TIP
Summarise the key points and use data to illustrate these.
Why? Because you will lose marks if you miss key points or fail to illustrate them.

IELTS Writing Task 2 #34

You should spend about 40 minutes on this task.

Write about the following topic:

In some countries it is thought advisable that children begin formal education at four years old, while in others they do not have to start school until they are seven or eight.

How far do you agree with either of these views?

Give reasons for your answer and include any relevant examples from your own knowledge or experience.

Write at least 250 words.

IELTS TIP

Include an overview of the information - either in your introduction or conclusion.

Why? Because you will lose marks if your answer does not contain an overview.

IELTS Writing Task 2 #35 (Answered)

You should spend about 40 minutes on this task.

Write about the following topic:

Today's teenagers have more stressful lives than previous generations.

Discuss this view and give your own opinion.

Give reasons for your answer and include any relevant examples from your own knowledge or experience.

Write at least 250 words.

IELTS TIP
Try to show that you can use your own words (wherever possible) and a range of grammatical structures.

Why? Because you will get more marks for vocabulary and grammar if you can do this.

IELTS Writing Task 2 #36

You should spend about 40 minutes on this task.

Write about the following topic:

Governments around the world spend too much money on treating illnesses and diseases and not enough on health education and prevention.

Do you agree or disagree with this statement?

Give reasons for your answer and include any relevant examples from your own knowledge or experience.

Write at least 250 words.

IELTS TIP
Divide your answer into paragraphs and use linkers to connect your ideas. Why? Because you will get more marks if you can organise your answer well and use a range of linking and reference words.

IELTS Writing Task 2 #37

You should spend about 40 minutes on this task.

Write about the following topic:

Many people believe that increasing levels of violence on television and in films is having a direct result on levels of violence in society. Others claim that violence in society is the result of more fundamental social problems such as unemployment.

How much do you think society is affected by violence in the media?

Give reasons for your answer and include any relevant examples from your own knowledge or experience.

IELTS TIP
Count your words to make sure you have written enough.
Why? Because short answers lose marks. (There are no extra marks for long answers.)

IELTS Writing Task 2 #38

You should spend about 40 minutes on this task.

Write about the following topic:

Compare the advantages and disadvantages of three of the following ways of learning a foreign language.

State which you consider to be the most effective.

studying on your own
taking lessons with a private tutor
taking lessons as part of a class
taking lessons online
going to live in a country where the language is spoken

Give reasons for your answer and include any relevant examples from your own knowledge or experience.

IELTS TIP

Make a quick plan either mentally or on rough paper. Decide on your main ideas.

Why? Because the examiner will be looking for a number of clear main ideas.

IELTS Writing Sample #39   (Answered)

You should spend about 40 minutes on this task.

Write about the following topic:

Should the international community do more to tackle the threat of global warming?

Give reasons for your answer and include any relevant examples from your own knowledge or experience.

Write at least 250 words.

IELTS TIP
Present your main ideas clearly and use examples to support them. Why? Because you will get more marks if your ideas are clear and well supported.

IELTS Writing Sample #40   (Answered)

You should spend about 40 minutes on this task.

Write about the following topic:

Genetic engineering is a dangerous trend. It should be limited.

To what extent do you agree?

Give reasons for your answer and include any relevant examples from your own knowledge or experience.

Write at least 250 words

IELTS TIP

Write a conclusion and re-state your position.
Why? Because your examiner will expect to find a logical conclusion and a consistent position.

IELTS Writing Sample #41

You should spend about 40 minutes on this task.

Write about the following topic:

In the past, shopping was a routine domestic task. Many people nowadays regard it as a hobby.

To what extent do you think this is a positive trend?

Give reasons for your answer and include any relevant examples from your own knowledge or experience.

Write at least 250 words.

IELTS TIP

Try to show that you can use your own words (wherever possible) and a range of grammatical structures.

Why? Because you will get more marks for vocabulary and grammar if you can do this.

IELTS Writing Sample #42

You should spend about 40 minutes on this task.

Write about the following topic:

A government's role is only to provide defence capability and urban infrastructure (roads, water supplies, etc.). All other services (education, health, social security) should be provided by private groups or individuals in the community.

Discuss both these views and give your own opinion.

Write at least 250 words.

IELTS TIP

Divide your answer into paragraphs and use linkers to connect your ideas. Why? Because you will get more marks if you can organise your answer well and use a range of linking and reference words.

IELTS Writing Sample #43

You should spend about 40 minutes on this task.

Write about the following topic:

Some people think that developed countries have a higher responsibility to combat climate change than developing countries. Others believe that all countries should have the same responsibilities towards protecting the environment.

Discuss both these views and give your own opinion.

Write at least 250 words.

Error Warning

Know = already have the information; find out = get the information.

Study = learn about a subject through books / a course: I'm studying law; I'm studying for my exams. We don't use any other prepositions after study. NOT I am studying about law.

Learn = get new knowledge or skills: I'm learning English; I'm learning to knit. Note that we say you are taking a course, NOT learning a course.

NB Prepositions after learn: learn about, learn from, learn to: I learned a lot from this course. NOT I learned a lot with this course.

IELTS Writing Sample #44

You should spend about 40 minutes on this task.

Write about the following topic:

Social media is becoming increasingly popular amongst all age groups. However, sharing personal information on social media websites does have risks.

Do you think that the advantages of social media outweigh the disadvantages?

Give reasons for your answer and include any relevant examples from your own knowledge or experience.

IELTS Writing Tip

In IELTS Writing Task 2 questions, when you write the main body of your essay, you need to explain your ideas fully. Examiners are looking to see how you develop your topic sentences, and will give you a better score if you do it well.

At the end of any type of essay in the IELTS exam, you need to write a short conclusion. The important thing to remember is there are no right or wrong conclusions, and the examiner will not make any judgements about your opinions, so write freely and clearly.

IELTS Writing Sample #45 (Answered)

You should spend about 40 minutes on this task.

Write about the following topic:

Nowadays many countries have very cosmopolitan cities with people from all over the world. How can the government ensure that all these people can live together harmoniously?

Give reasons for your answer and include any relevant examples from your own knowledge or experience.

Write at least 250 words.

IELTS Writing Tip

Task 2 of the General training test is an essay. Don't forget to plan your essay structure before you start writing. You should include an introduction, ideas to support your argument or opinion, real-life examples to illustrate your points, and a conclusion based on the information you have provided.

IELTS Writing Sample #46

You should spend about 40 minutes on this task.

Write about the following topic:

In many countries, very few young people read newspapers or follow the news on TV. What do you think are the causes of this?

What solutions can you suggest?

Give reasons for your answer and include any relevant examples from your own knowledge or experience.

Write at least 250 words.

IELTS Writing Tip

The band descriptors for this task penalise you for poorly organised answers. Although you may not be able to link points fluently it is important that you include some main ideas and that these are arranged in a logical order. The examiner should be able to distinguish between main and supporting points and should be able to follow the development of the answer.

IELTS Writing Sample #47

You should spend about 40 minutes on this task.

Write about the following topic:

Many people believe that formal "pen and paper" examinations are not the best method of assessing educational achievement.

Discuss this view and give your own opinion.

Give reasons for your answer and include any relevant examples from your own knowledge or experience.

Write at least 250 words.

ERROR Tip
Errors often occur when a letter is silent, for example in the words government, technology and otherwise. Be especially careful with vowel combinations in words such as beautiful and enormous. Also, remember to check that you have added any suffixes accurately: -ness and -ful are often misspelled.

IELTS Writing Sample #48

You should spend about 40 minutes on this task.

Write about the following topic:

Some people choose to eat no meat or fish. They believe that this is not only better for their own health but also benefits the world as a whole.

Discuss this view and give your own opinion.

Give reasons for your answer and include any relevant examples from your own knowledge or experience.

Write at least 250 words.

IELTS Writing Tip

'Agree or disagree' questions are the most common questions in both IELTS Academic and General Training modules. You can either answer them like a 'for and against essay', looking at both sides of the argument, or you can put forward your own personal opinion and take one side of the argument i.e. 'agree or disagree'.

IELTS Writing Sample #49 (Answered)

You should spend about 40 minutes on this task.

Write about the following topic:

Each year, the crime rate increases.

What are the causes of crime and what could be done to prevent this rise in criminal activity?

Give reasons for your answer and include any relevant examples from your own knowledge or experience.

Write at least 250 words.

Essay Tip
A good way to make your writing more stylish is to use some noun phrases in your essay. Noun phrases give the reader more information about a noun. For example, with the nouns prices or the Internet, you can make the noun phrases rising house prices or the invention of the Internet.

IELTS Writing Sample #50

You should spend about 40 minutes on this task.

Write about the following topic:

Modern communications mean that it's no longer necessary to write letters.

To what extent do you agree or disagree with this statement?

Give reasons for your answer and include any relevant examples from your own knowledge or experience.

Write at least 250 words.

FINAL Tip

Whatever the task, whether it is problem-solving, looking at effects or consequences, defending an opinion, comparing and contrasting evidence or ideas, you will need to evaluate.

Every essay will involve an evaluation of ideas. That simply means that you need to say whether an idea or concept is good or bad, or better or worse than another one.

ANSWERS :

TASK 2 # 27 SAMPLE BAND 9 ANSWER

Nowadays, supermarkets are stocked with food products from around the world. Some would argue that it would be better if food produce was not imported. I firmly believe that this view is correct, and will discuss the reasons why in this essay.

INTRODUCTION: Topic introduced and writer's opinion given.

It is certainly the case that importing food can have a negative effect on local culture. This can be seen in countries such as Japan where imported food has become more popular than traditional, local produce, eroding people's understanding of their own food traditions. Although some would claim that this is a natural part of economic development in an increasingly global world, I feel strongly that any loss of regional culture would be detrimental.

BODY 1: First idea plus examples for support. Describes what others may argue but refutes it by restating the writer's view.

A second major reason to reduce imports is the environmental cost. Currently, many food imports, such as fruit, are transported thousands of miles by road, sea and air, making the product more expensive to buy and increasing pollution from exhaust fumes. Despite the fact that the trade in food exports has existed for many years, I am convinced that a reduction would bring significant financial and environmental gains.

BODY 2: Second idea described rind explained. Opposing idea
given then refuted by giving the writer's view.

However, many jobs depend on food exports and some less developed countries may even depend on this trade for economic
survival. In spite of this, the importance of developing local trade should not be undervalued.

BODY 3: Short paragraph starts with an opposing view then refutes it.

In conclusion, I am certain that reducing food imports would have cultural and environmental benefits. What is more, the local economy should, in time, prosper commercially as the demand for local and regional products remains high resisting the
competition from overseas.

TASK 2 # 30 SAMPLE BAND 9 ANSWER

Most people would agree that car ownership has increased in recent years and is causing a range of problems, particularly in built-up areas. I think there are a number of ways that governments can aim to deal with this.

Many big cities in the world have traffic problems but these problems vary. For example, it is reasonably easy to drive around my city after 10 am and before 5 pm. However, outside these hours, you have to allow double the usual time to reach your destination. In some other cities, traffic is congested at all times, and there is the continual sound of car horns as people try to get wherever they want to go.

One of the best approaches governments can take in busy cities is to encourage the use of public transport. This means the transport facilities have to be well run and people must be able to afford them. Buses, trams and trains are good ways of getting around, and if they are cheap and reliable, people will use them.

Another approach is to discourage people from actually entering the city by building car parks and shopping centres on the outskirts. Many cities around the world do this quite successfully and offer passengers bus transport into the centre, if they need it.

At peak travel periods, governments can also run campaigns to encourage people to be less dependent on their cars. Apparently, a lot of car trips involve very short journeys to, say, the supermarket or local school. These are often unnecessary, but we automatically get in our cars without thinking.

Clearly we all have a responsibility to look after our cities. Governments can do a lot to improve the situation and part of what they do should involve encouraging individuals to consider
alternatives to driving.

TASK 2 # 35 SAMPLE BAND 9 ANSWER

Despite a continuing improvement in standard of living, many people believe that young people suffer more stress than older generations. In this essay, the arguments surrounding the issue of teenage stress will be discussed.

Firstly, teenagers are exposed to more products than earlier generations as a result of living in a modern consumer society. Through films and the media, they see celebrities with expensive jewellery, clothes and cars. In addition, youth-oriented advertising gives them an awareness of the latest technology such as digital music formats and mobile phones. Consequently, teenagers feel pressure to acquire these items. Some might argue that these pressures are not new. However, I believe that such stresses were not so strong during earlier times.

It could also be argued that pressures at school are stronger than before. In order to achieve the lifestyle they see in the media, teenagers must succeed in their studies so they can compete for the best jobs. Parental pressure, examinations and homework are all reported as causing increased levels of strain.

On the other hand, although it may be true to say that modern society produces certain stresses it does not necessarily mean that stress was previously absent. In earlier times, hunger and physical discomfort would undoubtedly have caused high levels of anxiety, as would hard physical labour, for example, working down a mine. Any balanced view must take into account these alternative factors.

To sum up, consumerism and academic pressures are powerful causes of stress on today's teenagers. Nevertheless, it is my view that these stresses are no greater than those experienced by earlier
generations of teenagers.

(267 words)

TASK 2 # 39 SAMPLE BAND 9 ANSWER

Global warming has long been recognized as a serious problem by most climate scientists. Governments around the world have begun to take the necessary measures to address it. However, as our understanding of the scale and nature of the problem is still developing, efforts to tackle global warming need to be reassessed from time to time.

Recent evidence suggests that some risk factors associated with climate change may have been overstated. Sea levels are now expected to rise by approximately one metre, not two metres, as previously thought. This is because some glaciers and ice sheets appear to be contracting, the Arctic, for example, while others, such as the Antarctic, appear to be expanding. Also, it is now thought that the Gulf Stream is unlikely to vanish. It may, therefore, be possible to scale back plans for flood defences in coastal areas.

However, there is also evidence that some of the consequences of climate change may have been understated. Tropical forests are now believed to be more vulnerable to drought. Hurricanes and typhoons may become more severe. Greater efforts should therefore be made to protect vulnerable populations, especially in tropical areas. Buildings in storm-prone areas may also need to be re-designed to withstand high winds.

These recommendations, however, address the symptoms of global warming, not the root cause: the generation of greenhouse gases. Whatever the precise scale and nature of the consequences of global warming, they are all undesirable. Clearly, more needs to be done to reduce the burning of fossil fuels. Stricter emissions targets should be set and use of alternative sources of energy encouraged. It would be profoundly irresponsible to do nothing about the causes of global warming.

TASK 2 # 40 SAMPLE BAND 9 ANSWER

Over the last few decades, remarkable advances have been made in the field of genetic engineering. Consequently, scientists now have the ability to manipulate genes for a range of purposes, from making improvements in agriculture to experimentation with human genes. The question, however, is whether there should be any limitations on this development. Is this essay, I shall examine both sides of the argument.

Firstly it is clear that genetic engineering has brought about certain benefits in terms of crop production. Now plants, for example, can produce more fruit more quickly. This achievement mean that greater harvests are guaranteed, so that more people can be fed. As for the impact of genetic engineering on healthcare, advocates claim it could be used to cure a range of health-related problems, such as cystic fibrosis and Alzheimer's. Children and adults with these diseases endure terrible suffering, yet with gene therapy, there is a possibility of a better quality of life.

Despite these advantages, there are some aspects of genetic engineering which require ongoing consideration. Critics claim that genetically modified plants have little nutritional value and that they will lead to the eradication of weeds, which many insect species depend on. In the case of gene therapy, it is still uncertain how the alteration of one gene, even though it may be faulty, could affect the functions of the human body in the long term.

In my opinion, the benefits of genetic engineering can outweigh the drawbacks, provided governments and scientists consider the consequences carefully, and put people before profit.

(256 words)

TASK 2 # 45 SAMPLE BAND 9 ANSWER

In today's cosmopolitan world it is unusual to find a major city or country where there are no immigrants. People travel more now than they ever did in the past and populations have had to adapt to this transitional lifestyle much more quickly than in the past. Ultimately society, as a group of individuals, directs the way that new arrivals in a country are treated. But the government can do a number of things to support this.

Firstly, all governments should insist that schools teach history and culture from more than one country, not just the home nation. By learning how others have lived we gain insight into alternative cultures and ways of life which makes us more accepting when we meet people from those countries.
Of course we don't have time to learn about the history of every country in the world but understanding at least one other culture opens our minds and makes us more tolerant.

In addition, when immigrants choose to settle in a country, the host government should offer free language and culture lessons. It is impossible for new arrivals to integrate if they do not understand the language and habits of their new home. I believe it is important for immigrants to learn the culture of the place they have chosen to settle. By acquiring the language and knowledge about the culture, they will be able integrate more easily and comfortably without necessarily losing their own identity.

Finally the governments of countries should make sure that they have some stringent laws to protect people from aggression or prejudice so that, should an immigrant face terrible attitudes, they have some protection. By ensuring people feel safe the host country shows that it is civilized and promotes integration.

In summary, understanding others is the key to harmonious living but laws should also be in place to protect people from those who can't behave responsibly.

(317 words)

TASK 2 # 49 SAMPLE BAND 9 ANSWER

The number of vegetarian in a community may depend on various factors, for example the traditions of the country, the wealth of the country, the religion or the age group. Therefore, the reasons why people choose to exclude meat and fish from their diet may also vary.

Some people become vegetarian because they believe that this will benefit their health. Undoubtedly, eating too much meat, especially too much red meat, is not to be recommended. Moreover, the fact that there are healthy populations in some parts of the world where no one eats meat proves that it is not, as some people claim, an essential part of the human diet. However, it is important to ensure that enough protein, for example, is included in the diet from other sources. Where vegetarianism is not a tradition, this may require some careful planning.

In my experience, it is quite common for people to become vegetarians because they feel that it is selfish to eat meat or because meat production increases global warming. They may also feel that if no one ate meat, there would be no food shortage, because meat production uses up food resources. This idealistic point of view is very attractive, but it is hard to judge whether it is in fact correct.

In some families, if a teenager decides to become a vegetarian they may do so partly out of a spirit of rebellion, because this behaviour can be interpreted as a criticism of their parents' way of life. However, provided that they continue to eat healthily, the parents should not raise objections, in my opinion. Vegetarianism is a valid choice in life. Moreover, research shows that vegetarians tend to be healthier in many ways than meat-eaters.

Personally, I think that being a vegetarian is a good idea in principle as there are proven health benefits and probably social benefits as well. However, it does not suit everybody, and I doubt whether it will ever be a universal choice.

(330 words)

TRANSITION WORDS

Transitional Words

This structured list of commonly used English transition words — approximately 200, can be considered as quasi complete. It can be used (by students and teachers alike) to find the right expression. English transition words are essential, since they not only connect ideas, but also can introduce a certain shift, contrast or opposition, emphasis or agreement, purpose, result or conclusion, etc. in the line of argument.
The transition words and phrases have been assigned only once to somewhat artificial categories, although some words belong to more than one category.

There is some overlapping with prepositions and postpositions, but for the purpose of usage and completeness of this concise guide, I did not differentiate.

Additive Transitions:
These show addition, introduction, similarity to other ideas, &c.
Addition:
indeed, further, as well (as this), either (neither), not only (this) but also (that) as well,
also, moreover, what is more, as a matter of fact, in all honesty,
and, furthermore, in addition (to this), besides (this), to tell the truth,
or, in fact, actually, to say nothing of,
too, let alone, much less additionally,
nor, alternatively, on the other hand, not to mention (this),

Introduction:
such as, as, particularly, including, as an illustration,
for example, like, in particular, for one thing, to illustrate
for instance, especially, notably, by way of example,

Reference:
speaking about (this), considering (this), regarding (this), with regards to (this),
as for (this), concerning (this), the fact that
on the subject of (this)

Similarity:
similarly, in the same way, by the same token, in a like manner,

Identification:
that is (to say), namely, specifically, thus,

Clarification:
that is (to say), I mean, (to) put (it) another way, in other wor

Adversative Transitions:
These transitions are used to signal conflict, contradiction concession, dismissal, &c.

Conflict:
but, by way of contrast, while, on the other hand,
however, (and) yet, whereas, though (final position),
in contrast, when in fact, conversely, still

Emphasis:
even more, above all, indeed, more importantly, besides

Concession:
but even so, nevertheless, even though, on the other hand, admittedly,
however, nonetheless, despite (this), notwithstanding (this), albeit
(and) still, although, in spite of (this), regardless (of this),
(and) yet, though, granted (this), be that as it may,

Dismissal:
either way, whichever happens, in either event, in any case, at any rate,
in either case, whatever happens, all the same, in any event,

Replacement:
(or) at least, (or) rather, instead

Causal Transitions:
These transitions signal cause/effect and reason/result, etc...

Cause/Reason:
for the (simple) reason that, being that, for, in view of (the fact), inasmuch as,
because (of the fact), seeing that, as, owing to (the fact),

Condition:
on (the) condition (that), granted (that), if, provided that, in case,
in the event that, as/so long as, unless, given that,
granting (that), providing that, even if, only if,

Effect/Result:
as a result (of this), consequently, hence, for this reason, thus,
because (of this), in consequence, so that, accordingly
as a consequence, so much (so) that, so, therefore,

Purpose:
for the purpose of, in the hope that, for fear that, so that,
with this intention, to the end that, in order to, lest
with this in mind, in order that, so as to, so,

Consequence:
under those circumstances, then, in that case, if not,
that being the case, if so, otherwise

Sequential Transitions:
These transitions are used to signal a chronological or logical sequence.

Numerical:
in the (first, second, etc.) place, initially, to start with, first of all, thirdly, (&c.)
to begin with, at first, for a start, secondly,

Continuation:
subsequently, previously, eventually, next,
before (this), afterwards, after (this), then

Conclusion:
to conclude (with), as a final point, eventually, at last,
last but not least, in the end, finally, lastly,

Digression:
to change the topic, incidentally, by the way,

Resumption:
to get back to the point, to resume, anyhow, anyway, at any rate, to return to the subject,

Summation:
as was previously stated, so, consequently, in summary, all in all, to make a long story short, thus, as I have said, to sum up, overall, as has been mentioned, then, to summarize, to be brief, briefly, given these points, in all, on the whole, therefore, as has been noted, hence, in conclusion, in a word, to put it briefly, in sum, altogether, in short,

Conjunctions

Cohesive Devices

A variety of useful English Conjunctions exists, which complete this list of the most used Cohesive Devices. Together, they can help to express a cohesive view and easy understandable and readable texts.

There are three basic types of conjunctions:

Definition
coordinating conjunctions
used to connect two independent clauses
subordinating conjunctions
used to establish the relationship between the dependent clause and the rest of the sentence
correlative conjunctions
used to join various sentence elements which are grammatically equal
Coordinating Conjunctions
Comes usually in the middle of a sentence, and a comma is used before the conjunction (unless both clauses are very short). They join individual words, phrases, and independent clauses.
Whereas coordinating conjunctions join parts of a sentence, the purpose of transitional words and phrases usually is to join two 'sentences'.

Examples:
We can draw lessons from the past, but we cannot live in it. [Lyndon B. Johnson]
The purpose of most computer languages is to lengthen your resume by a word and a comma. [Larry Wall]

And, but, for, nor, or, so, and yet — are the seven coordinating conjunctions. To remember them, the acronym FANBOYS can be used.

F = for

A = and

N = nor

B = but

O = or

Y = yet

S = so

Subordinating Conjunctions

Also called subordinators, introduce a dependent clause. These adverbs that act like conjunctions are placed at the front of the clause - and a comma is needed at the end of the adverbial phrase when it precedes the main clause.

Examples:
If the only tool you have is a hammer, you tend to see every problem as a nail. [Abraham Maslow]
Some people make headlines while others make history. [Philip Elmer-DeWitt]

Conjunctions Concession

though
although
even though
while

Conjunctions Condition

if
only if
unless
until
provided that
assuming that
even if

in case (that)
lest

Conjunctions Comparison

than
rather than
whether
as much as
whereas

Conjunctions Time

after
as long as
as soon as
before
by the time
now that
once
since
till
until
when
whenever
while

Conjunctions Reason

because
since
so that
in order (that)
why

Relative Adjective

that
what
whatever
which
whichever

Relative Pronoun

who
whoever
whom
whomever
whose

Conjunctions Manner

how
as though
as if

Conjunctions Place

where
wherever

Correlative Conjunctions

They are always used in pairs and denote equality; and show the relationship between ideas expressed in different parts of a sentence - and thus make the joining tighter and more emphatic. When joining singular and plural subjects, the subject closest to the verb determines whether the verb is singular or plural.

as . . . as
just as . . . so
both . . . and
hardly . . . when
scarcely . . . when
either . . . or
neither . . . nor

if . . . then
not . . . but
what with . . . and

whether . . . or
not only . . . but also
no sooner . . . than
rather . . . than

Conjunctive Adverbs

They are often used as a linking device between ideas. They show logical relationships expressed in clauses, sentences or paragraphs. Conjunctive adverbs are very emphatic, so they should be used sparingly.

Similar to And

also
besides
furthermore
likewise
moreover

Similar to But

however
nevertheless
nonetheless
still

conversely
instead
otherwise
rather

Similar to So

accordingly
consequently
hence
meanwhile
then
therefore
thus

Idiomatic Expressions

What are idioms?

Definition

An idiom (also called idiomatic expression) is an expression, word, or phrase that has a figurative meaning conventionally understood by native speakers. This meaning is different from the literal meaning of the idiom's individual elements. In other words, idioms don't mean exactly what the words say. They have, however, hidden meaning.

Examples

"Kick the bucket"
"Spill the beans"
The meaning of these expressions is different from the literal meaning or definition of the words of which they are made. Their meaning are however used figuratively. They mean respectively:

"to die "
"to tell people secret information"

IDIOMATIC BANK:ANIMAL

a little bird told me
said when you don't want reveal the source of your information.
Example(s):
"How did you know the news?"
"Oh, a little bird told me."

as gentle as a lamb
Said about kind, innocent, mild-mannered people.
Example(s):
She is as gentle as a lamb. That's why everybody likes her.

be a chicken
be a coward.
Example(s):
Don't be a chicken. Talk to her about your love for her.

shoot the bull

The phrase shoot the bull means to chat and gossip.
Example(s):
The old ladies often get together and shoot the bull.
The boss fired them because he found them shooting the bull instead of doing the job they were paid for.

make a monkey out of
make a monkey out of
(also make a fool out of someone) to cause a person, group, or action to appear foolish or inferior; to subject someone or something to ridicule.
Example(s):
Don't make a monkey out of me. You'll regret it.

dark horse
The phrase dark horse is an idiomatic expression that refers to a usually little-known person who unexpectedly wins or succeeds, especially in a competition of some sort.

IDIOMATIC BANK: HEALTH

be full of beans
said about someone who is active, lively, healthy and has a lot of energy and enthusiasm.
Example(s):
He's always full of beans when he goes to work.

black out
to lose consciousness.
Example(s):
He blacked out when he fell.

nurse someone back to health
to look after a sick person until he recovers.
Example(s):
He is fortunate to have such a caring wife. She was glad to nurse him back to health.

safe and sound
safe and without injury or damage.
Example(s):
The kids returned from the excursion safe and sound.

hale and hearty
in a good health.
Example(s):
In spite of her old age, she looks hale and hearty.

a clean bill of health
said when you examine someone or something and state that they are healthy, in good condition, or legal.
Example(s):
1. The president was given a clean bill of health by his doctors.
2. The company received a clean bill of health because it fulfilled all the safety requirements.

IDIOMATIC BANK: TIME

against the clock
To work or race against the clock means to do something as fast as possible and try to finish it before a deadline.
Example(s):
The students were racing against the clock to finish the paper before the deadline.

any minute soon now
(also any moment/second/time now) very soon

Example(s):
The news about the president's resignation will be broadcasted on TV any moment now.

caught in a time warp
The phrase to be caught in a time warp is an idiomatic expression that means to remain unchanged from a time in the past although everything else has.
Another variation of this idiom is to be stuck in a time warp or to be in a time warp.
Example(s):
The town seems to be caught in a time warp. People there are living as if they were still in the middle age.

for the ages
The phrase for the ages is an idiomatic expression that refers to something that will be memorable and noteworthy; standing the test of time.
Example(s):
His speech wasn't a speech for the ages. It was barely a speech for the evening.

in the nick of time
The phrase in the nick of time means at the last possible moment, just before it's too late.
The word nick refers to a notch, cut, or indentation on an edge or a surfac
Example(s):
I arrived at the train station in the nick of time and took the last train to t capital city.

IDIOMATIC BANK: TIME

once in a blue moon

The phrase once in a blue moon is an idiomatic expression that means not very often or very rarely.
Blue moon refers to an additional full moon that appears very rarely during a year.
The phrase has nothing to do with the actual color of the moon. It just means that something happens very rarely.
Example(s):
Once in a blue moon, her husband brings her a gift.
She sees him once in a blue moon.

stand the test of time

If something stands the test of time, it lasts for a long time.
Example(s):
Their marriage has stood the test of time.

Rome wasn't built in a day

Said to emphasize that great work takes time to do. Nothing of importance can be done in a short period of time.
Example(s):
Don't expect immediate outstanding earnings fom your new buisiness. Rome wasn't built in a day.

time flies

The phrase time flies means that time passes very quickly especially when you're having fun.
Its Latin origin is tempus fugit
Example(s):
Time flew while they were talking about the old beautiful days.

under the wire

At the last minute; before the deadline; barely on time; nearly late.
Example(s):
He turned his report just under the wire.

high time

If it's high time you did something, it is the appropriate time for it.
Example(s):
It's high time you began learning how to drive.

IDIOMATIC BANK: LAW

above suspicion
This phrase is used to describe a person who is honest enough that no one would suspect.
The origin of the phrase is attributed to Julius Caesar, who divorced his wife Pompeia, on the grounds of her possible involvement in a public scandal, saying that "my wife ought not even to be under suspicion." This gave rise to a proverb, sometimes expressed: "Caesar's wife must be above suspicion."
Example(s):
That guy is a peaceful man; he is above suspicion.

hold someone accountable (for something)
to consider someone responsible for something.
Example(s):
I hold you accountable for whatever happens to my daughter.

in the eyes of the law
legally.
Example(s):
In the eyes of the law you are not allowed to treat people like that.

Justice is blind
This expression means that justice is impartial and objective. There is an allusion here to the Greek statue for justice, wearing a blindfold so as not to treat friends differently from strangers, or rich people better than the poor ones.
Example(s):
No matter who you are, you must respect the law. Justice is blind!

the long arm of the law
This idiomatic expression refers to the far-reaching power of the authorities or the police.
Example(s):
Don't try to escape! The long arm of the law will catch you wherever you may go.

law unto oneself
This idiomatic expression describes a person who behaves in an independent way, ignoring rules and what is generally accepted as correct.

IDIOMATIC BANK: LANGUAGE

at a loss for words
If you are at a loss for words, this means that you are unable to speak.

This phrase is mainly used when you are stunned to the point of speechlessness.
Example(s):
She was at a loss for words when she saw the golden ring that her husband bought her for their marriage anniversary.

it goes without saying
The phrase it goes without saying is an idiom. It refers to something that is so obvious that it is needless to say it.
Example(s):
It goes without saying that you have to wake early tomorrow morning if you want to participate in the marathon competition.

it's all Greek to me
The phrase it's all Greek to me is an idiom in English, referring to something that is not understandable.
for mine own part, it was Greek to me. I could tell you more news too: Marullus and Flavius, for pulling scarfs off Caesar's images, are put to silence. Fare you well. There was more foolery yet, if I could remember it.
(William Shakespeare, The Tragedy of Julius Caesar (1599))

talk a mile a minute
The phrase talk a mile a minute is an idiomatic expression that means to speak very fast; to talk in a very quick or hurried manner.
Example(s):
I can never follow everything he's tries to say. He talks a mile a minute.

talk is cheap
The phrase talk is cheap is a proverb that means it is easier to say you will do something than to actually do it.
Example(s):
My elder brother promised to help me with my homework, but talk is cheap.

IDIOMATIC BANK: MONEY

a dime's worth
an insignificant amount
Example(s):
At best, he'll make a dime's worth of difference with his interference in the affair.

all that glitters is not gold
appearance is sometimes misleading. Things that appear valuable or worthwhile might not be as good as they look.
Example(s):
The house looks beautiful from the outside but the inside part of the house looks terrible; all that glitters is not gold.

come into money
If you come into money, you get some money unexpectedly, usually by inheritance.
Other variants of this idiom:
come into some money
come into a small fortune
Example(s):
He came into a lot of money.

make a fast buck
(also make quick buck) to earn money without much effort.
Example(s):
If you have got any idea of how to make a fast buck, please tell me!

strapped for cash
The idiom strapped for cash to be short of money.
Example(s):
I'm strapped for cash, can you lend me ten dollars?

save money for a rainy day
The phrase to save money for a rainy day is an idiomatic expression that means to reserve money for a time when it might be needed unexpectedly.
Example(s):
A good manager has to save a little money for a rainy day.
I Kept some extra money for a rainy day.

IDIOMATIC BANK:MONEY

quote a price
state in advance the price for...
Example(s):
The mason quoted a price of 500$ to fix the roof of my house.

money talks
money talks suggest that with money people can get whatever they want.
Example(s):
She got what she wanted. Well you know money talks!

minting money
(also minting money) Earning a lot of money quickly.
Example(s):
Since the arrival of the new manager, the restaurant is minting money.

licence to print money
if a company or activity is a licence to print money, it generates a lot of money without much effort.
Example(s):
Advertizing companies are just a licence to print money.

ill-gotten gains
money or other possession gained dishonestly.
Example(s):
All his ill-gotten gains are hidden somewhere in his bedroom.

drop a dime
to drop a dime means to make a phone call, usually calling the police to inform on or betray someone.
Example(s):
He went out to drop a dime on John.

for love nor money
said when it is difficult to get something or persuade someone.
Example(s):
You can't get help for love nor money these days.

IDIOMATIC BANK: LIFE

all walks of life
Occupations, roles, social class, or lifestyle.
Example(s):
Those who attended the wedding represented all walks of life.

larger than life
Very imposing, renowned, or impressively influential.
Example(s):
He is such a special man; somewhat larger than life.

you can bet your life
This idiom is used to mean that you are absolutely certain that something is true or will happen.
Example(s):
You can bet your life they'll get married.

give the kiss of life
To give the kiss of life means to help a person who has stopped breathing by giving them artificial respiration, that is to say, by blowing into their mouth and pressing their chest.
Example(s):
He saved a victim of an accident by giving him the kiss of life.

live on borrowed time
The phrase is used to describe a person who continues living when everybody expected him to die.
The origin of the phrase
This idiom refers to time borrowed from death as if death was a person.
Example(s):
All the doctors that he visited informed his family that he was going to die soon. But against all odds, he continued living on borrowed time.

low-life
(Also lowlife)
A low-life is a person who is considered morally unacceptable by their community such as thieves, drug dealers, drug users, alcoholics, thugs, prostitutes and pimps.
Example(s):
I saw him with a bunch of lowlifes.

IDIOMATIC BANK: LOVE

aching heart
The phrase aching heart is an idiomatic expression that refers to the feeling of pain because of love.
Example(s):
My aching heart is telling me that he doesn't love me.

match made in heaven
The phrase a match made in heaven refers to two people, so well-suited to each other that their marriage is likely to be happy and successful.
The phrase may also refer to a very successful combination of two people or things.
Example(s):
As soon as they met, they liked each other and decided they should get married. They were really a match made in heaven.

misery loves company
The phrase misery loves company means that if someone is miserable, they like others to be miserable too so that they can feel better about themselves.
Example(s):
I see that you got into a lot of trouble, but since your colleague is in trouble too, that makes you feel better. Misery loves company, doesn't it?

misery loves company
The phrase misery loves company means that if someone is miserable, they like others to be miserable too so that they can feel better about themselves.
Example(s):
I see that you got into a lot of trouble, but since your colleague is in trouble too, that makes you feel better. Misery loves company, doesn't it?

send love to someone
The idiom send love to someone refers to an affectionate greeting or message given to someone.
Example(s):
Lisa sent her love to all the family.

love at first sight
An instantaneous attraction
Example(s):
It was love at first sight when we met.

IDIOMATIC BANK: RELATIONSHIP

bad blood
unpleasant feeling between different people.
Example(s):
There is bad blood between Nancy and Leila. They are rarely in good terms with each other.

affinity for
said about you have attraction , preference or sympathy for something or someone.
Example(s):
He has an affinty for classical music.

be an item
said about a couple when they are having a romantic relationship.
Example(s):
I heard that Leila and Joe are an item.

blood is thicker than water
family relations are more important than all other relationships.
Example(s):
Even if Nancy and her brother often argue, they always forgive each other. Blood is thicker than water.

go with the flow
To do what people do and accept things as they are.
Example(s):
Don't worry too much! Take it easy and go with the flow!

play a joke
(also play trick) to deceive someone for fun.
Example(s):
On April fool's day some people play practical jokes on their friends.

raw deal
said when someones is ill treated.
Example(s):
Mary got a raw deal. She was innocent, but she had to pay a big fine.

IDIOMATIC BANK: RELATIONSHIP

the mother of all
an extreme example which is the biggest, most impressive, or most important of its kind.
Example(s):
Failure is the mother of all success.

father figure
The phrase father figure usually refers to an older man who is respected and who is characterized by power, authority, or strength.
Example(s):
The kids respected him as a father figure.

get on like a house on fire
said about two people like each other and become very close friends in a very short time.
Example(s):
The two ladies are getting on like a house on fire.

good fences make good neighbors
(also good walls make good neighbors) this means that people should respect other people's property and privacy and mind their own business.
Example(s):
Our neighbor should prevent his children from messing up our lawn. Good fences make good neighbors.

IDIOMATIC BANK: WORK

work your fingers to the bone
to work extremely hard.
Example(s):
He works his fingers to the bone to help his five children grow up in a healthy environment.

break your back
If you break your back to do something, you work very hard to do it.
Example(s):
I am not going to break my back to this job for such a low salary.

bean counter
An accountant.
Example(s):
The company is hiring a new accountant.

back to the salt mines
If you go back to the salt mines, it means you have to return back to the workplace.
Example(s):
The vacation is over. Back to the salt mines!

cold piece of work
If someone is a cold piece of work they are difficult to deal with.
Example(s):
Did you see how she treats her husband? She is a cold piece of work.

burn the midnight oil
Work hard, especially late into the night.
Example(s):
She was burning the midnight oil preparing for her daughter's wedding when she had a heart attack.

shoot the works
to spend all the money you have or to try as much as you can to do something.
Example(s):
We shot the works on our son's education.

IDIOMATIC BANK: WORK

devil finds work for idle hands to do
People are inclined to do frivolous or harmful things to get rid of their boredom when they don't do anything useful.
Example(s):
My husband made sure that the children are always occupied doing something because you know the devil finds work for idle hands to do.

dirty work
(also do the dirty work) unpleasant work or dishonest action.
Example(s):
1. I don't know but I feel there is some dirty work going on in this company.

get the sack
to be dismissed from employment.
Example(s):
Because he was always late, he got the sack.

gum up the works
The phrase gum up the works means to prevent a process, a system or a machine from working smoothly.
Example(s):
He is not careful enough and always gums up the works.

hustle and bustle
The phrase hustle and bustle refers to a busy activity usually in a noisy surrounding.
Example(s):
I don't like the hustle and bustle of big cities.
I need to have a break from the hustle and bustle of the big city.

labor of love
The phrase labor of love refers to a work that brings you great pleasure.
Example(s):
John helps street children get basic education as a labor of love.

sweat blood
to work very hard.
Example(s):
He sweats blood every day just to bring home the bacon.

IDIOMATIC BANK: TRAVEL

at the wheel
Driving; in control of a vehicle.
Example(s):
You know he fell asleep at the wheel. They were so lucky they didn't have an accident.

desert a sinking ship
The phrase desert a sinking ship means to stop being involved in a situation because failure is imminent.
Example(s):
She knew it was time to desert a sinking ship because she had read all the reports about the catastrophic financial situation of the company.

bad news travels fast
The phrase bad news travels fast means that news about misfortune and trouble circulates quickly.
The phrase 'ill news spreads apace' is another idiom which has the same meaning.

drive someone up the wall
To irritate or annoy someone; to make a person very angry or bored; to infuriate.
Example(s):
Her persistent nagging drove me up the wall.

fifth wheel
Anything superfluous or unnecessary.
Example(s):
I felt like a fifth wheel when they started looking at each other affectionately.

flight of fancy
If your idea is described as a flight of fancy, it is an imaginative but entirely unrealistic idea.
Example(s):
I had a flight of fancy of becoming a champion of the world in boxing in spite of my weak body disposition.

IDIOMATIC BANK: TRAVEL

highways and byways
major and minor roads.
Example(s):
They spent their holiday exploring the highways and byways of the country

hit the road
To begin traveling; to leave a place; to go away.
Example(s):
1. We've got a long way to go. Let's hit the road to make it by sunset.
2. It's time for me to hit the road; it is getting late.

live out of a suitcase
The phrase to live out of a suitcase is an idiomatic expression that means to stay very briefly in several places, with only the belongings in your suitcase.
Example(s):
I travel so much and am always living out of a suitcase.

my way or the highway
This expression is used to say that people have to do what you say; otherwise, they will have to leave or quit the project.
Example(s):
He has a "My way or the highway" approach to leading his government and his party.

miss the boat
To fail to take advantage of an opportunity.
Example(s):
The price discount ended yesterday and I just missed the boat on a great deal

jump on the bandwagon
To profit from a craze; to join a trend.
Example(s):
After the incredible success of the new product, the company has jumped on the bandwagon, and released a new version of it..

IDIOMATIC BANK:SPORT

a lost ball in the weeds
The phrase a lost ball in the weeds refers to a person who is completely lost or confused and does not know what they are doing, how to do it or possibly even where they are.
Example(s):
I got confused as to what I should do. I was a lost ball in the weeds.

ball of fire
a person who is especially hard-working, high-achieving, ambitious, or active.
Example(s):
They say he is a real ball of fire. He has already demonstrated his wish to climb higher.

be new to the game
The phrase to be new to the game is an idiomatic expression that refers to a lack of experience in a particular activity.
Example(s):
I can't teach this class. I have never had any training in teaching mathematics. I am new to the game.

come down on somebody like a ton of bricks
to hit or punish somebody.
Example(s):
I'll come down on you like a ton of bricks if you do that once again!

the ball is in someone's court
When the ball is in someone's court they have to take action.
Example(s):
The ball is in your court now. You should decide what you want to do.

track record
The phrase a track record is an idiomatic expression that refers to a person or organization's past performance in any type of endeavor.
Example(s):
They have a strong track record in creating successful websites.

IDIOMATIC BANK: MUSIC

strike a chord
If something strikes a chord with you, it reminds you of something, it seems familiar to you or you are interested in it.
Example(s):
That woman struck a chord with me. It seems to me that I had seen her before.

What does all that jazz mean?
Meaning of idioms with examples...
all that jazz
Everything else related to something; and other similar things.
Example(s):
They enjoyed the party: cocktails, dancing, and all that jazz.

blow one's own horn
(also toot one's own horn) to brag; to talk boastfully.
Example(s):
Nancy likes to blow her own horn.

carry a tune
The phrase to carry a tune means to sing a melody accurately.
Example(s):
I can't carry a tune, but my sister sings very well.

clean as a whistle
If someone is as clean as a whistle they are perfectly clean.
Example(s):
She's clean as a whistle.

draw in one's horns
(also pull in one's horns) to become less impassioned, aggressive, or argumentative; to back down from a fight; to yield or capitulate.
Example(s):
He wanted to fight again but we managed to calm him down and get him to draw in his horns.

IELTS Band Scores

9 Expert user:
has fully operational command of the language: appropriate, accurate and fluent with complete understanding.

8 Very good user:
has fully operational command of the language with only occasional unsystematic inaccuracies and inappropriacies. Misunderstandings may occur in unfamiliar situations. Handles complex detailed argumentation well.

7 Good user:
has operational command of the language, though with occasional inaccuracies, inappropriacies and misunderstandings in some situations. Generally handles complex language well and understands detailed reasoning.

6 Competent user:
has generally effective command of the language despite some inaccuracies, inappropriacies and misunderstandings. Can use and understand fairly complex language, particularly in familiar situations.

5 Modest user:
has partial command of the language, coping with overall meaning in most situations, though is likely to make many mistakes. Should be able to handle basic communication in own field.

4 Limited user:
basic competence is limited to familiar situations. Has frequent problems in understanding and expression. Is not able to use complex language.

3 Extremely limited:
conveys and understands only general meaning in very familiar situations. Frequent breakdowns in communication occur.

2 Intermittent user:
no real communication is possible except for the most basic information using isolated words or short formulae in familiar situations and to meet immediate needs. Has great difficulty understanding spoken and written English.

1 Non-user:
essentially has no ability to use the language beyond possibly a few isolated words.

0 Did not attempt:
No assessable information provided.

Manufactured by Amazon.ca
Acheson, AB

16751076R00096